Snow-capped Mountains and Black Bears

Edited by **Pauline Rowe**

Words and Poems in Celebration of the
Gifts of Age and Survival

The Mossley Hill Writing Group

First published in Great Britain in 2016
by **North End Press**
an imprint of North End Writers
Old School Site, Lister Drive, Liverpool L13 7HH

Edited by Pauline Rowe

Typesetting by Pauline Rowe
Printed by Qwikprint, Bootle, L20 9DN

Cover illustrations by Thelma Thomas

North End Writers

"I have known the inexorable sadness of pencils" Theodore Roethke

Charity no 1118597
Company no 05927469
www.northendwriters.com
e: northendwriters@gmail.com

ISBN 978-0-9933466-0-6

CONTENTS

CONTENTS *continued*

It Ought to be Lovely to be Old

Self-Portraits related to Age and Experience

Letters about Ourselves

CONTENTS *continued*

CONTENTS *continued*

PREFACE

The Mossley Hill Writing Group met in February 2014 for the first of 10 weekly workshops on the timely theme of *The First World War at Home*. Group members (aged between early 50s and 90) are all service-users of Mossley Hill Community Mental Health team at Mersey Care NHS Trust in Liverpool.

The First World War project produced so much discussion, ideas and writing that we celebrated with our own performances and readings in the Summer, a highlight of the work being our reading for the Association of Cognitive Analytical Therapists (ACAT) conference at Liverpool HOPE University in July. We also did a reading on the War theme at Central Library, Liverpool for World Mental Health Day. The initial aims of this project were to build confidence and creativity, share knowledge, enable inclusion, improve quality of life and increase wellbeing. Within 6 months our members were sharing their work with an international audience of psychologists: more importantly we developed our own small community of people who took time to listen, discuss and share not only writing for the page but words of friendship and mutual support.

Our work has continued through the partnership of Mersey Care NHS Trust and the Liverpool charity North End Writers. In Autumn 2014 we met for our second writing project *The Gifts of Age* which continued until the Summer 2015. One of our inspirations was the poem *Beautiful Old Age* by D.H. Lawrence, which ends with the following lines:

And a girl should say:
It must be wonderful to live and grow old.
Look at my mother, how rich and still she is! –

And a young man should think: By Jove
My father has faced all weathers, but it's been a life!

We spent time considering our own lives especially in their riches and experiences of facing all weathers. This book includes a range of writing, poems and letters that grew from this contemplation.

Writing can be a serious and enriching way to engage with the world we inhabit and ourselves: this has been the experience of the Mossley Hill Writing Group.

Pauline Rowe

Mersey Care **NHS**
NHS Trust

Poet-in-Residence
December 2015

Looking at
Our Younger Selves

Kath Harper

___

A Taste of India

They speak in tongues these people
these adults, this mum and dad.
Exotic throwaway lines;
perhaps one day I'll be an A graduate translator.

Or maybe a master criminal,
who creeps stealthily with intent
to steal away the treasures
hidden in that room.
In that dresser, in that drawer.

Or a No 1 detective
who chews on her pipe, hat on head,
says "yes" a lot, then through a series
of clues unlocks the mystery.

No, I'll be a great explorer,
climb that wooden hill,
force away the boulder that covers the cave,
find the mystery within a mystery.

A large cask with several drawers;
and one which holds such wonders –
images of far away places,
snow-capped mountains and black bears.

A group of tanned young men, in uniform.
Perhaps a familiar face?
I must investigate but dare not ask.

My dad's drawer with its key.
A coin, a workhouse penny,
papers with a name –
a name I know so well.

A soldier in exotic places
with beautiful women
in places of trouble
and places of sun.

Margaret Kempson

Blondie-Margo

My hair was very fair and in fact my Dad used to call me 'Blondie-Margo.' I remember that the skirt I was wearing was made from an old skirt belonging to my mother, who was a very good seamstress, she never wasted any material. I seem to remember that I was also the tallest girl in the class. I used to walk to school with my brother David and my sisters Ada and Gladys.

If it rained we all wore macs and sou'westers and wellingtons. We had to take a peg to school to clip our wellingtons together. We had to put our name on the peg. Woebetide you, if you forgot your peg, as the teachers would be cross. The school has now been knocked down but still exists in another location. It is still called Lister Drive.

Margaret Kempson at 6 years of age (school photograph)

Thelma Thomas

A Different Time

Looking at this photo of my younger self – a different time and place. Who am I? Expectations by other people – too much responsibility: always had to think about what others needed and I felt like 2 people – the adult child and the fun child (who I had to bury deep inside).

Not a happy home, I never felt I belonged. No space, as the rooms were small. And gas mantles, which I always seemed to break, being tall for my age.

Cutting newspaper into squares and threading on string for the outside toilet. Taking the acid battery to get topped up for the wireless. My brother, 14 months younger, always cried at everything, always hanging on to me wherever I went. He liked collecting bugs in the bedroom, to keep in a matchbox.

The old mattress under the stairs where we slept when the bombs started dropping; going into the yard afterwards to see the red and orange sky – dust everywhere, and the strong smell of burning houses and wood, the bangs and bright flashes like lightning in the sky.

Next day collecting wood to burn on the fire and lighting candles when it went dark again. We moved from this house when I was 11 years old in 1948.

Colette Williams

Four years old

Away from Mum and Dad and siblings, visited once a week. A nurse's cloak to keep my shoulders warm. Hospital haircut – just look at the fringe! Ribbon bows – care of Mum. A pad and pencil – I must have liked to draw. And hospital sheets – 50 shades of grey.

Kath Harper

The Child

Summer's warmth and giggles with friends whose preference is
tadpoles and mud.
Mother's calling, it's teatime, come quickly or else.
Is it liver and onions?
My favourite; the smell, it lingers and brings a rumbling tum and
happy smiles.

The cold, the snow, numb fingers, numb legs, numb everything.
Janet, my friend next door but one, always in trouble!
What did they do with that pond? The frogs? The newts?
Houses on my field. Poor cows. Poor sheep.

Annette Butler

Two Photographs

The two photographs (both black and white) are separated by 65 years.

The little girl (two and a bit years old and thin for my age) poses on a sunny day. This would be summer 1949 and was taken, I believe, at the Torquay guesthouse where we usually holidayed. We did not have a dog, so having one sitting comfortably near was an added element. I look up on that day, viewing the relatively small world which all youngsters inhabit – for me a secure one within the parameters of my small family: Mum, Dad, Sister and – until I was eight – my maternal Grandmother.

As an adult one tends to look back wistfully, wishing that youthful naivety could last longer. Particularly, that certain events had not happened so early, if at all. If only the ghastliness of much teenage and early 20s years could have been avoided! Being a square in a round hole, easier to be in the crowd or a duo (if the other half accepts you, angst and all), but individuality to be valued alongside selfhood. Quite a lot of tears and fears, as well as good things. We didn't have Facebook as an instant means of sharing me-him/me-her, 'my new best friend' with a superficially interested audience. Back then your own self and sometimes family would have to do and usually, meaningfully, did.

I see an older, wiser person in the current photograph. So very much time separates the two images: now the OAP hardly recognisable (apart from hair) looks back at the little blonde girl. No facial lines on the tiny girl, unfortunately quite a lot on the adult woman. In the current photo I'm looking over my shoulder, waiting to read. Reading is what I've been doing for much of my life. I am still looking, enjoy challenge and meeting new people, often annoyed at physical limitations.

As the wonderfully acerbic American writer Dorothy Parker said:

Oh life is a glorious cycle of song
A medley of extemporanea
And love is a thing that can never go wrong,
And I am Marie of Romania.

from '*Not so Deep as a Well*'

Peter Cookson

Who is this?

Who is this chubby four-year-old who stares so solemnly and suspiciously at the camera wielded by Harry Hedges in his photographic studio on Church Road? Can it be the same person in the later photos that mark out stages in his life? - at the start of big school and about to move into higher studies – on the edge of

9

manhood – always with his three brothers, all taller and more handsome.

My own best dateable memory is of my fourth birthday. It was a sweltering July day. The little boy in his white linen suit, white blouse and pale blue shorts, has not a care in the world. Each day is complete in itself. Yesterday is forgotten already. Tomorrow doesn't exist.

To my contemporary photo

What has brought you to this?
Bald pate, shrunken cheeks, downturned mouth, scrawny neck.
In one word, life.
But it has been a good life, worthwhile.
There have been many more kindnesses than hurts;
Wonderful experiences; lifelong friends; loving family.
What more could you ask for?
Not that it was always easy.
The studies were long and hard but there were compensating pleasures.
Responsibility was a burden that at times nearly broke you
but people were understanding and you came through.
There were mistakes but very few that did anyone harm.
People now say to me: *you deserve the leisure of retirement*
But I remain to be convinced. Life seems empty
Without a job to do – watching "Flog It" on television –
But people don't seem to mind. They take you as you are.
So much to be grateful for, so many people to thank.

Childhood
Memories

Thelma Thomas

Hub of noise, New Year

One, a piece of coal – another a slice of bread, a few coins to another, an orange. It's snowing. The step to the house is covered. We open the entry back door, pushing snow with our feet then off we go, to walk around to the front of the house, footprints, paw-prints from dogs. Give a knock on the front door and let in the New Year.

Peter Cookson

'Childhood Ideogram'

This poem takes me back to my first days of nursery school – the Kindergarten run by the nuns on Mount Pleasant. Sister Winefried, big and buxom, whose capacious bosom could heal any hurt. The impossible task of learning to tie a bow. The nativity play in which I was to play a shepherd and entered the scene too soon and was sent back behind the curtain in confusion. Oh happy days! But unhappy ones too, for the sorrows of childhood are as real as any adult ones.

Note: *Childhood Ideogram* is a poem by Larry Levis and can be read here - http://www.poetryfoundation.org/poem/177467

Colette Williams

Outside it's snowing

Christmas Eve, early to bed
new PJs cannot sleep
Downstairs the sound of paper wrap
Who is Santa – this dear old chap
does he exist?
All goes quiet, footsteps on the stairs
Bedroom doors squeak open
Pillowcases stuffed with toys,
books and other things,
pretend to be asleep, well
for a little while.

Ralph Killey

I place my head upon the desk.

The door flew open to my past.
I learned of China from a friend
And how my father met his end.
Your brain sometimes goes wild.
All this escapes you as a child.
And then it changes back unheeded.
An old school desk is all that's needed.

Annette Butler

Childhood Ideogram – Memories

Memories of Junior School fairly vivid; much more so than in Infants: only about 10 minutes walk away – nobody was taken by car – not so many parents even had one.

It was a Victorian school, red brick of course and basic even by the standards of the 1950s as it had outside toilets and, I think, no Hall for assembly. There was one classroom for each year, four in all, 8 years to 11 years. The first years were taken by elderly Miss Smith who was beloved of all of us. There were probably between 25-30 in each class. She came in every day in her Austin Ruby car (or similar vehicle) from her village about 18 miles from our semi-rural school and had done so for about 30 years.

I walked to school on my own from age 9, usually choosing the route that took me over a stile surrounded on one side by a large farm and smallholding with our housing estate on the other. So quiet and I loved reading and writing and Miss Smith who, unlike the 2nd year teacher was so polite and fair. Happy Days!

Ged Daley

Childhood

I think of my childhood, happy days, a very close family and many close friends then I grew older and most of them have gone but in my mind they all live on. Days at the beach and camping in Wales, follow the leader and many more games.

Margaret Kempson

Childhood Memories

When I started school, we had to learn to use pen and ink. I remember going home with ink splashes on my clothes, which made my mother cross. The school caretaker used to go from classroom to classroom with a large jug of ink, to enable him to top up the inkwells. When I started secondary school in 1940, inkwells and pens were still in use.

In fact when I started work at 16 years of age in 1945 we had to use black pencils or fountain pens. It wasn't until Lazlo Biro invented the ballpoint pen, in 1947, that pen and ink was gradually phased out over a number of years.

Little Pigs Have Big Ears

Kath Harper

Little Pigs Have Big Ears

What a well-worn phrase used to silence a conversation, a conundrum. No pig in the room, what does she mean? I suppose little pigs do have big ears, that much is true but why tell dad now?

My Mum, a lovely Lancashire woman through and through, used the quaintest sayings often with no meaning, often totally out of context to my young mind. Some of these now totally defunct:
It's like Muldoon's picnic in here! Can we say that today without sounding prejudiced? My dad was of Irish stock, she meant no offence.

I'm not struck. Why not say what you mean? That they're not your cup of tea? Funny Mum, a quip for every occasion.

She's no better than she should be. *It's all my eye and Peggy Martin.* Mmmm – do I know this person and what has it to do with her and my Mum's eye? Perhaps there'll be "tears before bedtime". She was right about that one. A psychic. Yes, Mum was right about lots of things. How life whizzes by, how unimportant some things can be and yes, little pigs do have big ears – but I'm not telling.

Thelma Thomas

Little Pigs Have Big Ears

How very often I was told this by my Grandmother (we called her Nannie Rose) always when she was talking to my mother or someone she met on the street that she knew and I was with her. I used to hide on the stairs to listen in, as neighbours used to pop in and out of each others houses having cups of tea and a good

17

gossip. Hence the saying – little pigs have big ears. One time still stays with me to this day when I overheard my Nannie say to my mother about Hitler maybe landing in England and what would we do if he did? My mother said – I will gas all the kids before he comes to save him the jobs. I did wonder at the time what his job was. But I never asked.

Peter Cookson

Seen and not heard

My childhood was spent against the background of wartime and the years of austerity that followed the war. We were brought up to be frugal. The family wasn't poor compared with our neighbours on Durning Road, but every penny was counted. Not that there was much to spend it on. Most things were still on coupons long after the war. We were brought up to turn off unnecessary lights – a habit that has stayed with me all my life and drives my younger colleagues mad. Four inches of water was all that was permitted in the bath – though how they expected to enforce the law makes the mind boggle.

The days followed one another undifferentiated except for the regular occurrence of Sundays. Sunday morning was for church – "don't fidget" followed by the great treat of my 'Sunday pint.' I had been befriended by one Harry Sefton, proprietor of the newsagent and sweet shop across the road from our house. I spent many happy hours sitting on the counter in his shop chattering away - an innocent relationship that would raise eyebrows these days. After early Mass Mr Seston (as I called him) would take me on the 11a bus to Fairhaven Lake where we would visit the Lakeside café and he would buy me a glass of lemonade while he drank a coffee. This was the up side of Sunday.

18

The downside was that Sunday afternoon was dedicated to visiting elderly relatives. This involved sitting still on horsehair chairs in the front parlour while our mother talked endlessly to grandma or great aunt.

It Ought to be Lovely to be Old

Ralph Killey

It Ought to be Lovely to Be Old

It ought to be lovely to be old
And I find it so
No-one doing what you're told
By bosses who pretend to know.
Kids are happy, settled down
No more worries there,
Peace and quiet, sit and think
On your favourite chair.

House is yours, mortgage gone
Everything is peace
And yearly holidays
In our lovely Greece.

Ged Daley

Then reality kicks in.

All our experience counts for nothing as youth has all the answers. The body won't work like it used to, when kicking a ball is a distant dream, running for buses is a thing of the past, and the pensions we worked for no longer last. But happiness is still mine to behold as the people I have met have made it worthwhile. Most of my friends bring me a smile.

Annette Butler

The word 'lovely' is not one too many of us would use to describe old age. "Ought" could mean a younger person thinking how age should feel many years ahead. But surely no period of age is ever the ideal; personal health and mobility gets nearer to a good state. However, luck and the lack of it often interferes with people enjoying it. Those able to embrace new things, be a joiner – U3A (University of the Third Age) is very popular, with widows tending to outnumber widowers and bachelors. Short and perhaps long-distance travel is possible with many tours tailored to 'Seniors'. But, of course, some escapes and experiences are easier for the more affluent.

Colette Williams

It ought to be lovely to be old
Not for me, it's lonely and cold
Surrounded by people, but yet
So alone,
My only pals the TV and phone.

I dread the day and wish it away.
The night brings terrors
and broken sleep,
memories of wounds
run very deep.

Margaret Kempson

It ought to be lovely to be old but not everybody enjoys old age. Some people can be troubled with ill health, caused by dementia, arthritis, cancer and lots of other complaints. On the plus side, many of these people can be helped by therapy, various operations and walking aids. On the contrary, it is nice to be old if you have good health and are pain free. Also, on the plus side, you can be helped across the road, even if you don't need any help. Sometimes you can be offered a seat on a crowded bus but not every time. I think old age on the whole can be a time of contentment - at least it is in my case.

Mo Thomas

It ought to be lovely to be old. It really should be lovely to be old but not for all with old age problems and pains in the knee, not able to walk, stuck in the house, no one to run a message. But for me, as I'm not very old - in fact, I think I will stay with the same age, 21. Who cares? It's just a number; it's the feeling and outlook of how we grow old. My ageing body is not doing too badly at the moment. I prefer my life now to when I was a younger married mum, too hard – long hours, constant work, demands from others and being a person who found it hard to say no. If I had been an octopus with all those arms it would have come in handy!

Peter Cookson

'It ought to be lovely to be old'….

'Ought to be'… but is it?
Sometimes yes, sometimes no.
Blessed are those who reach old age
In relative good health
With friends and family still around them.

Loving and being loved makes all the difference.
A continuing sense of usefulness is vital.
It doesn't necessarily involve a lot of activity
But the experience of being valued just for being.

Note: the writing in this previous section was inspired by the poem
by D.H. Lawrence *Beautiful Age* and its first line
"It ought to be lovely to be old." (A copy can be read here:
http://www.poemhunter.com/poem/beautiful-old-age-2/)

Self-portraits related to Age and Experience

"and all the darknesses are dared…"

Elizabeth Jennings

Kath Harper

Perhaps a little light shines through
the years of struggle and regret.
A light not extinguished, a kindness,
a love of living things
through eyes that have seen pain.

You made it along a road
deep with travail,
no bomb could explode
your love for others.

Peter Cookson

An honest portrait reveals the soul.
It dares to reveal the hidden corners of a life lived through a
multitude of experiences, good and bad. The painter's self-portrait
is the highest form of this art, since he alone knows the full truth
and, if he has the skill, can capture it in paint.

26

Colette Williams

And all the darknesses are dared
your jeans are '60s, very flared,
your hair looks good, I like the back.
Go to work like that you'll get the sack.

Silver threads amongst the gold
must get my roots done.
Hair falls out from every place
but grows well upon my face
Tweezers out must pluck my chin.

Annette Butler

The challenges of life. As you get older, at least in my case, I try to plan a little way ahead and not waste too much time in idle contemplation. There's a need to fill in time with things I like doing and meeting up regularly with those who also want to use their minds – thinking, writing, creating. I used to have a tendency to live through others. Not now.

I usually avoid the mirror – too much information via my facial lines on how many years have passed. I met an horrendous darkness 2012-2013, whilst gradually appreciating many, many visits from wonderful family and friends who could always see the light just ahead.

27

Margaret Kempson

All the darknesses are dared, but seeing a portrait of myself recently, which my sister passed on to me, I hardly recognized it as I looked so glamorous at age 18 years. Now, gone is the lovely blonde hair, the smooth wrinkle-free complexion, the sight has deteriorated and I now have to wear spectacles.

However, old age has its compensations, no mortgage to pay, get up any time you like, and attentive daughter and son-in-law and a lovely grand-daughter who is the apple of my eye.

Why Did Rembrandt Paint Eighty Portraits of Himself?

Sandra:
Was it because he was self-indulgent? Was it because he wanted to know what he looked like when he had grown older. How many people bought his paintings?

Ralph:
To paint a self-portrait I would find very difficult. However, Rembrandt did many. I think he was trying to eradicate and lower his feelings of insecurity. Also he may have needed to look and see that even as he aged his gift was still intact.

Margaret:
He possibly had an inferiority complex about his looks and could have felt that by painting so many portraits he could disguise his imperfections in a skillful way. In those days there were no mobile phones therefore he could not take "selfies" as so many people do nowadays. However, his paintings could be called a 'portrait-fit' not a photo-fit. With so much modern technology these days, it is

doubtful whether a modern day artist would do the same. However, his portraits are unique.

Peter:
Perhaps he couldn't afford a model or perhaps he had no commissions and wanted to keep his hand in. But more likely there was a deeper motive: the search for his inner self; the desire to perpetuate himself; a fascination with the effect of time on the human face; the eternal search for the perfect likeness.

Pauline:
because he could never get his eyes right
because he wanted to use up his paint
because he thought it would keep him going in the winter
because it gave him something to do
because it kept him out of his wife's way
because it helped him to avoid doing household chores
because he wasn't worried about impressing his patrons
because he wanted to create a legacy
because he could not believe the face God had given him

Letters about Ourselves

Sandra Taylor

Outside it's snowing.
Images in my mind.

The inkwells with bright ink –
it got on my hands.

Colette Williams

Inspired by the film Philomena
Dear Philomena,

I think you're great. Life was so very tough, to have a child, a lovely boy who was taken from you to another land. Doesn't seem like he had a very happy childhood or adolescence. A clever lad (who did very well), a high achiever but he had to keep a secret. To be homosexual at that time….he contracted AIDS and sadly died. He'd looked for you back home in Ireland but was misled. Dying, his last wish was to be buried in the graveyard of the convent. I think he knew you'd find him there and you did.

Colette

PS Just one question – what's a good swipe of shite??

Ralph Killey

Dear Ralph,

I saw your picture this morning in *The Times*. I must say, old friend, life has taken its toll. However, you are not alone. I wouldn't have the confidence to have my countenance appear unadorned in public as I now resemble the map of Madras.

Keep going, my friend. Your humour helps me through the day, as you know with whom I have to spend my time.

Your friend,
Elizabeth R

Margaret Kempson

Dear Paula,

This is a photograph of me taking part in a group reading about World War 1 at the Central Library in the Autumn. We studied the War for several months and as well as Central Library we did the same readings at Hope University for an international conference, and at Mossley Hill hospital.

We gained insight into what life was like at that period, such as rationing owing to food shortages, the postal system and how 12 million letters were posted every week for the forces. At home many women worked on the land and munitions factories and also did a lot of jobs formerly done only by men.

What a pity that when the war ended they lost those jobs, as they had to step aside and let the men take their jobs back.

It wasn't until 1975 that women could earn as much as men and do mostly the same jobs as that was the year of the Sex Discrimination and Equal Pay Act.

Aren't you glad that you were born at the right time to reap the benefits of the above?

Lots of love,

Mum

Thelma Thomas

I am looking at the photo of me at the present time wearing my Lumie band that Roxanne, my Great Grand-daughter made for me. She is 4½ years old.

Where has time gone?

I look quite happy and bright but I feel sad and lonely at times. I miss the very close relationship with my husband and all the things we did as a couple: walking in the hills, camping and touring in our old mini-bus right around the coast of Scotland. We used to have a good laugh.

Remember the trip we did going to Iceland? It was only for a day flying from Liverpool. It was really good, swimming in the Blue Lagoon.

And the great laugh in the all together in the dressing room......

Kath Harper

Kathleen Ann,

That was a most enjoyable morning spent with your new friends. You need friends and you've found a few gems here.

I think you know the value of others and hopefully they can see the compassion you hold so dear. Beneath the noise and talkativeness lies a caring heart. You have struggled and do struggle but you're still here. You're doing OK. Stop worrying.

It's hard to look at this photo. Is it vanity or a desire to be younger? Maybe a touch of melancholy for years gone by; mum, dad and kids.

Ged Daley

Prior to getting married my life was worry free. No responsibilities, close family and no commitments. I gave my mother half my wages and pub landlords and record shops the rest.

Then I met Nita. Life was still good. But at 25 it was time to grow up and start taking on some responsibilities, paying bills, somewhere to live and thinking of others. You forget that gas and electricity are not free. Beds don't make themselves and the kitchen is not only for cleaning your football boots (which always got me into trouble). I did not know then that it was the start – a long learning curve.

Childhood Sundays

Colette Williams

It's 8 o' clock I think I'll get up. The smell of bacon ascends the stairs. Grandma's cast iron frying pan, sizzling hot, Dad in charge (he liked to cook): None for us, not before 10 o'clock Mass. Fr McNamee was very strict. Mum's around. Busy day. School uniforms washed and ironed. In the summer months a trip to the local farm shop – rhubarb or a cabbage, lots of fun. Cows coming back for milking just in time to see them PLOP!

Radio on. Two-way Family Favourites. Jean Metcalfe made us laugh. FAZACURLY and AGUEBIRTH. Sunday lunch always a roast. Table set, starched linen cloth, knives with bone handles, my twin brother Paul scanning the plates just to make sure he had the biggest roast potatoes – careful Paul, mum is getting cross.

After lunch we'd play outside, Mum washed up, Dad in his chair snoring – he must be tired. My sister Margaret bakes a cake, 'Mary Baker', nice for tea. 5 pm the Ovaltinees – we'd sing along. Time for bed before too long – school tomorrow. Have a bath. Read for a little but not too late.

Ged Daley

My Sundays as a child were for family and going to visit my grand-parents. In the Summer it was days at the beach or open air swimming pools. There were quite a few in those days. The cold water took your breath away but once in they were great fun.

38

Ralph Killey

Childhood memories

My Grand-dad and grandmother were my parents, due to the intervention of the second world war. Pleasures were few – but one pleasure was a visit to my uncle John, whose house was in Rock Ferry on the other side of the river. This incident I am about to relate occurred on such a visit.

My grandmother and I did the wonderful trip, tramcar – boat – tramcar – to uncle John's house. Then after a delightful afternoon we left to make our own way home. It was then something unusual occurred. My Gran said: 'would you like a lemonade?" 'Yes, please," I replied. We sat in the restaurant. Suddenly there was an enormous BANG! I screamed: "What was that Gran?" She replied, "It's a bomb, dear." War, by then, was our way of life. "Elbows off the table!"

Annette Butler

Childhood Sundays

I had the average childhood Sunday that I would imagine our family shared with most of our neighbours and, indeed, the country. Except, in our case, there was no extended family to visit or join us in a meal on that 'day of rest'.

Churchgoing was much greater in the 1950s and into the 60s than it has become over the rest of my life. As young children my sister and I attended Sunday School in one of the classrooms of our Infants School, which was only up the road. Because we were on a newly built estate no actual church was yet built. That building and its varied activities came when I was about 10, and was 'neutral' Congregational (now part of United Reformed).

My Mum had been a three-times-a-day attender at her family's Methodist chapel in Oldham, Lancashire, about 180 miles away. I believe all 5 children, Mum being the youngest, sang in the Chapel choir, and at least one of them a Sunday School teacher from about the age of 14. Growing up in Cheltenham my sister and I enjoyed the usual Sunday School treats of an annual Summer outing by coach, the nearest seaside being Weston-super-Mare, about 70 miles away, with its famously far-off-sea. But there was always the likelihood of a donkey ride. As we got a little older we girls – friends from Sunday and day School – joined the "Morris Dancers" - in fact a simpler version of the American-style Majorettes, where we marched around in our short white skirts and some kind of jacket to live music. I think that this was provided by either an older girl or adult, beating a drum. Meanwhile we all carried a little baton with tassels, our legs and arms supposedly synchronized as we stepped and twirled through our 'dance' routines. Sadly we didn't follow the North-West custom of Whit/Whitsuntide Sunday or Monday: children dressed in white, girls carrying floral symbols of Whitsuntide, boys carrying evergreens walked a set route. Brass bands, I think, accompanied them and picnics followed. A simpler age. My maternal grandmother could recall in her childhood attending her Primitive Methodist chapel where if a preacher was so moved, even excited by the word of God, he would sometimes jump the rails separating the body of the chapel from the preaching space. Nothing so exciting for us!

My experience of Sunday was less demanding of time needed to properly observe religion. In common with parents and grand-parents our Sunday School consisted of a short Bible story geared to the age group's attention span. Often, individual little books of Baby Jesus and Jesus ministering to children. Also the Miracles: Jesus Parting the Red Sea, Loaves and Fishes etc, these we took home to be read to us by Mum and Dad and, as we got better at reading, ourselves. We always crayoned and sometimes painted pictures of Bible stories at Sunday School – I don't remember any felt-tips – think they hadn't been invented yet. In my memory teacher was always a lady, or a girl, of about 18. We sometimes got stars for our artistic efforts and annually awarded prizes for our attendance.

We always sang – gosh, how we sang! (with appropriate hand gestures):

Yes, Jesus loves you
Yes, Jesus loves you
The Bible tells me so
And *Jesus wants me for a Sunbeam.*

Then back to lunch – our Dinner – with Mum finishing the preparation to the sound of the wireless on the Light Programme; my Dad probably reading the paper, helping arrange dishes and cutlery, and making the gravy for the Sunday roast. Roast meat was the great staple of British week-end life, unless you were that very odd thing, a Vegetarian. Also, fascinating for younger people is that chicken was then something of a luxury – confined in our house to Easter and only one or two other times a year. Women invariably did the cooking then. We always sat together as we had the meal and, in many homes, a grace preceded it. As my Dad was a confirmed non-believer, that bit never happened. The radio would be playing "With a Song in my Heart" as intro to Two-way Family Favourites. Also the familiar comedy programmes of the time often made my parents laugh a lot, particularly Round the Horne, The Navy Lark, Beryl Reid as schoolgirl Marlene etc., As we got older my sister and I delighted in the wonderfully distinct voice of Kenneth Williams, in particular Kenneth Horne, Betty Marsden etc. The innuendo passed over us as young children, with full enjoyment coming rather late.

My maternal grandma, who came to live with us at some point after her husband died, was pushed by our parents and us children in her wheelchair on Sunday afternoons in our local park, with her usually holding the bag of old bread to feed the ducks. We always wanted to see the swans, too. Very occasionally we'd go to the local Pub if dinner was going to be later than usual and sit in the beer garden, gran drinking a Mackeson's, my parents something similar, while we children had lemonade and crisps. This would have been absolutely frowned on by my parents and grand-parents beliefs in sacred, quiet Sundays. In my youth and working-class background it was very unusual to eat out and pubs mainly provided alcohol with 'food' coming in the form of a scotch egg, perhaps a dreary Ploughman's Lunch and crisps. There was also no loud *musak* or one-armed bandits to distract and take your money; generally a masculine escape from the world. As we had no car until I was 11 we walked, cycled or went by bus everywhere. My home town is in a valley and it takes a while to get to real hills, and certainly no wild places. In contrast my Mum (when younger), with friends and siblings, went often for shorter walks out to Saddleworth Moor, with longer walks on Sundays, weather permitting. They sometimes even drank unpasteurised milk bought straight from the farm to accompany their picnics!

My Dad, growing up in Newcastle, when I was about 13 or so started cycling out to the Northumberland coast where he could enjoy castles, sea and fresh air.

My husband Chris in Edinburgh could easily climb up Arthur's Seat, famous landmark of Salisbury Crags within minutes of the city centre. His family did not do Spiritual Sundays.

Brenda Roberts

Childhood Sundays

Sunday always seemed a lazy, leisurely day. It started late with a full English breakfast while the radio droned on about stuff that went right over my head; then an interminable weather forecast for shipping: Dogger, Fisher, German Bight…these are the names that have stuck in my head to this day.

Breakfast was no sooner over than it seemed to be lunchtime; one stomach can only take so much.

If the weather was fine usually a walk to Otterspool was on the cards. I don't know why, but I never felt happy there. Sefton Park always had a bright atmosphere, but I could never enjoy the long, long walk down Jericho Lane – which seemed about five miles

42

to such little legs – just to end up walking along a promenade looking at a dirty grey river. However, I didn't want to spoil the illusion of what a good little walker I was, as it seemed to please my Mum and Dad so much.

What I did prefer was the occasional trip to Hale Village. I used to enjoy the bus ride, particularly as Speke was left behind, and countryside took over. The thatched cottages were a delight to see, and you could buy bunches of flowers which they always seemed to have for sale. I can still remember their great smell, they were lavender and pink mostly. There was a sweet shop called *Immints and Deakin,* which certainly wasn't the least favourite part of the trip. They sold Duncan's Chocolate bars that had five different fillings, and as you bit each piece, pink strawberry would turn into bright orange which then became yellow pineapple, then green lime and raspberry to finish. Delicious rainbow bars, I called them. After that we'd begin to walk down to Hale lighthouse – funny how my little legs didn't feel tired on that walk. The air was clear and fresh, and I loved walking through fields of high grass and ears of barley or wheat or whatever, on the way down to the remote looking lighthouse. I suppose the sporadic nature of the Hale visits added to the attraction.

I enjoyed Sundays so much more in school holidays because in term time, once it got to about 5 o'clock, I'd get a miserable sinking feeling of dread at the thought of the new week starting.

All in all, Sunday was different, a day set apart from the rest and I try to keep it that way myself. I avoid hustle and bustle, and take a rest from the telly apart from a couple of special things.

Margaret Kempson

Childhood Sunday

In the 1930's I lived in the West Derby area of Liverpool with my parents, grandma and my three sisters and a brother. My father was in the police force and, depending on what shift he was on, he took us to various places on a Sunday, usually in the mornings. A typical Sunday would start with us all getting up early, having breakfast, usually consisting of porridge, bacon and egg and tea.

We would then get a tram to the Pier Head and then a ferryboat to Egremont. We then played on the sands there until it was time to make our way home. On a Sunday my mother always cooked a lovely roast dinner with home made apple pie to follow.

Shortly afterwards we would make our way to Sunday school which was held in Roscoe Ballantyne school hall. When we got there we played in the garden until tea was ready, which consisted of sandwiches, cakes, tinned fruit and cream and a cup of tea.

After tea we all sat around the table and played various games such as ludo, snakes and ladders, dominoes, draughts and various paper and pencil games and finally general knowledge. At that time my father was studying for his sergeant's examinations in the police force. One aspect of that examination entailed having a good grasp of general knowledge. Therefore we bought three General Knowledge books that he tested on the family regularly, which at the same time meant that he was improving his own general knowledge too.

Before going to bed we were given a cup of cocoa and two biscuits.

Other places we visited on a Sunday morning were Woolton Woods, Newsham Park, Croxteth Hall Gardens and Larkhill Gardens. Tram fares were cheap in those days, as children could get a penny return and adults a cheap transfer ticket which was a boon as not many people had their own cars at that particular time.

Letters to the Young

Dear Susan,

This letter may come as a surprise, possibly it is provocative but hopefully it will be of some interest. Please read what I have to say and if, at the end, you feel it is worthless tear it up and never give it another thought.

You might be asking yourself what does a 60 year old woman know about me. Yet I was 14 once and I probably have a greater memory of that time than I do about things which happened 12 months ago. Just one of the joys of getting older.

I am not writing to preach at you, that would be wrong of me but to help you think about yourself, your actions, your friends and the effect you have on each other and those around. Can you put yourself in someone else's shoes for a short time? I'm guessing you can as you're a smart girl with high intelligence; it should be a breeze. You seem to be a leader, someone who appears strong and does not cry easily. Life is to be lived, everything is fun or so it seems. I wonder if everyone in your circle of friends feels the same? Perhaps they have their own secrets that they do not share.

I'd like to tell you about a girl of 14 I once knew. She was tall for her age, overweight yet still pretty and eager to please the charismatic leader of her group of friends. When things were good they were very good. They went to school together, all clever girls, spent leisure time together and fancied boys together (sounds like bliss). Well for this girl it was not always the case. There was a dark side to this friendship, times when power was wielded over the others, times when all agreed with the word of one girl. Her friend who was loyal and kind was always the scapegoat, someone who carried all the blame, took all the knocks and still came back for more. She was miserable 80% of the time, waiting for the next ostracism or verbal abuse of physical attacks by a third party (made to ingratiate herself with the 'leader').

Often this lonely girl would go home and cry in her bedroom, a giant hole in her stomach, with a sense of anticipation for the next reprieve. As you will know, Susan, life can be very confusing for a 14 year old girl. Personally I couldn't quite decide whether I was child or woman, I resented being told what to do, yet always needed mum and home. Safe and sound. Home can be such a sanctuary, it can also be a prison or a place where we don't feel happy or safe.

Often people who hurt others do so because they're hurting too. They lash out not knowing what to do with their feelings, they're unhappy and confused. You may have heard the saying *kick the cat* – but, as I think you know, this sense of relief lasts for a short time only. Soon we feel the same as before and look for something or someone to punish.

The girl I knew never told anyone about her tormentor until she was much older. Her 'friend,' the leader of the gang got into lots of trouble, became pregnant and had to leave school at the age of 15. She stopped tormenting…

Susan, we each have within us a good nature – kindness, caring and understanding…but we also have the capacity to harm, to be cruel and unkind. Sometimes the unkindness gets the attention where none exists elsewhere. I ask you to think about all I have said. You're a girl who has much to offer, so much more than picking off friends. Please find someone you trust who you can talk to and find something you really enjoy doing then you'll start to feel differently about the attention you receive.

I read a quote recently, I can't remember where I saw it or who said it but it goes: *you will never reach the summit whilst knocking someone down.* As a much older person I can tell you this is true. Please take time to think.

Your friend,

Kath

Dear Joan,

Just a letter to outline a few things that might be helpful to you; the shows mostly start at 7.30 pm. I will meet you outside the theatre at 6.45 pm as you will always have to be ready to start half an hour before the curtain goes up. We will go up to the top floor to the wardrobe and the wardrobe mistress who is over us dressers. Back stage is very noisy with people coming and going with doors banging and lots of shouting – a bit like a railway station when a train comes in. When you meet the 'in-house' wardrobe mistress we will be told who we are dressing and which floor we will be on. As you're just starting it will be the chorus on the top floor – number 4. This job will be like no other job you've done before. You will be quite nervous. I will take you to the dressing room to meet who we will be dressing and on entering I will say "Hello, my name is Thelma and this is Joan – we will be your dressers for the week (or run)." You could be dressing men or women. You will have to get used to nudity but hopefully the lads will have their jocks on. The women are always topless but you will get used to it after a while. Pantomime is much harder with a lot of rehearsals that can go on into the early hours. That's the time the producer will make cuts and alter things; it will be very busy with everybody running around with lots of swearing, things to be let out and taken in. Just let it go over your head. You will learn to listen to the music as all your cues are taken from that and every dresser is dressing differently from you.

Here are a few things which will help and you will get used to hearing – every theatre all over the country will use them even in the big shows in London.

When you hear *a quarter to curtain* – at that point everybody you're dressing should be starting to move, you will have laid out the opening costumes on the backs of their chairs.

Five minutes to curtains – you must have them all laced up, or buttoned up or hooks and eyes – also they will write their names in lipstick on the mirror in the place where they sit.

Overture and beginners – that's it, down to the stage, they know where they are going, one mad dash, run your eyes over them – have they got gloves, feathers etc?

Prompt side is the nearest side to the dressing rooms.

Op-side is across to the other side of the stage. If you have a dress change on Op-side you have to go across under the stage and lay out your costumes there. You only have to see to costumes - wigs and props are done by other people. At the end of every show everything has to be hung up on hangers and you have to collect the laundry for wardrobe which will be bras, pants, gloves, fishnets. For men – it will be shirts, gloves, jocks. Another point – if the lads are talking in groups just ask them for their jocks- they will just take them off (very wet and sweaty) while you stand there. But wardrobe – that's you – can't go home til all the laundry is gathered in which will take at least half an hour after curtain. This is just a small insight into the job. You will learn as you go.

Best wishes,

Thelma

Colette Williams   *Letter to a Would-be Nurse*

Dear Sweet Heather,

So lovely to hear from you and your intention to train as a nurse. I'm tempted to begin my advice by saying *in my day...* but instead I will quote a definition of nursing that I heard from a lovely Nurse Tutor, Mr Harry Rose:

Nursing is doing for the patient what they cannot do for themselves, whilst encouraging them to do what they can. And that's exactly it. Of course today the role of the nurse has extended to include tasks previously only performed by the doctor. However a really good nurse should know when she *needs* the doctor, not that she wants to

49

be one. I fear that the extended role has been developed at the cost of attention to principles of good basic care.

Patients need to be treated with respect and dignity. They need to be clean and comfortable, nourished and well hydrated.

What I would advise you is try to spend a year or two before you start your training (if you can) working as a cadet nurse when you have the chance to learn the basics and learn them well. These will stay with you forever and can be readily applied to most situations.

Time spent with patients is so very important. You can learn so much from them. Always remember you are their advocate, ready to speak when they are unable and always find the courage to challenge opinion as your patient's life might depend on it.

Finally, enjoy your training, develop your sense of humour, that's not to say be flippant but there will be times when laughter can help.

Always remember I am here for you. With lots of love,

Great Aunty Colette

PS. In response to your anxiety around your male patients – with your equine background it should pose no problem, although I'm yet to met a man with the proportions of a stallion.

Sandra Taylor   _Letter to a Young Actor_

Dear Friend,

If you have to wear a costume or wig you must practice and practice with it so it is not foreign to you, especially if you have a period part, the ladies with their fans, the gentlemen with their long sleeves and cravats.

You must, above all, feel the emotion of the character. It's very important to take notice of the Director. If you listen you will learn.

Dear Colleague,

When I was a student for the priesthood in the seminary, the local parish priest used to come in once a week to lecture us in Pastoral Theology. The only words of his I recall concerned life in the presbytery, the parish house. They were these: "On Friday night the housekeeper takes her bath" and "Always use the lavatory brush."

My own advice to you as a newly-fledged priest would be less down-to-earth, but I hope useful none-the-less.

Don't take yourself too seriously. Still today many people hold the priest in high esteem. Don't let it go to your head or start throwing your weight about. Treat everyone with equal respect. There is a practice in the Royal Navy whereby a padre assumes the rank of a person he is talking to, be it admiral or able seaman. It's what St Paul calls "being all things to all men."

Never throw away a good sermon. It will come in useful three years hence, when the same Scripture readings come round again – and the congregation will be none the wiser. But don't use the same jokes or anecdotes because they are the one thing the people *will* remember.

Finally don't expect a lot of obvious results from your efforts. Leave it to the Lord to work behind the scenes. Your life will not always be easy, but it will bring you great consolations.

Ever yours,

Fr Peter

Annette Butler   *Advice to a young woman considering*
                                    becoming a parent

Dear Flora,

First of all think very, very carefully. Your life will change enormously.

By 'young' I'm thinking of someone between 24-35 years of age, not a teenager. I believe that people should keep their care-free years as long as they can. It is a huge responsibility to have a child and you will experience a wide range of emotions: stress, lack of sleep, often exhaustion, anxiety, the needs of a baby wholly dependent on others. But also the remarkable bond between the child and parent, the reciprocal love and surprises. You may well discover hidden talents and hitherto unknown patience!

Parenthood has also changed dramatically in the last 25 years or so with the advent of IVF (in vitro fertilization) for women with conception failure, also attitudes towards surrogacy for those wealthy or desperate enough. Anonymous donor insemination is widely available. Previously the 'pill' to prevent unwanted pregnancy and control conception. More familiar now are lesbian couples using a friend's sperm (often a gay man's) to create a child who might have 3 parents rather than 2. Gay couples can create a child with a gay or straight female friend. I know my mum, had she lived long enough, would have been shocked at some of this. Even The Archers has tackled the theme of donor insemination – in the story of Helen's pregnancy (Helen is often attracted to unreliable men.) Personally I hope you will bring up your child with a partner who **is** reliable. Consistency and real love for the child is truly the most important element.

If you can't conceive please seriously consider adoption or fostering. I was at school with several Dr Barnardo's girls. I know how they wanted to live in a real family home. Some of the girls were confused at not being orphans and occasionally seeing a parent (usually mother) who went away again, generally unable to have her daughter at home because 'home' was often chaotic and father not around. Up to the mid 70s an organisation called *the Society for the*

Unmarried Mother and her Child typified judgemental attitudes. I have known two families who successfully adopted, although not without difficulties. Agencies now are prepared to consider fostering or adopting older children of mixed or different race to the carers. Such nurturing requires great patience, energy, sympathy and sense of humour. Unlike natural parenting this may well mean one of you will have to put your career on hold according to the child's age and needs. But you will certainly be able to cope and really make a difference to that person.

Looking forward to your reply,

Your always,

Annette

Ralph Killey

You Can Do It Friend

If you want to be a writer,
and you say you do,
I am going to try to help you
to try to see you through.

You must employ your senses -
touch, sight, sound, taste and smell.
Always study people,
watch them very well.

Get yourself a notebook
next time you're in Town.
When a thought occurs to you,
simply write it down.

Always have the courage
to write what your heart sends,
this part isn't easy
and you'll find you lose some friends.

Be ruthless when you read your work
it must be true to your belief
I'll try to guide you on your way
and never plagiarise, that causes grief.

Here is an example,
a piece that I have written,
I hope you really like it,
and like me you will be smitten.

Moonlight

Slowly, silently now the moon walks the night in her silver shoes.
This way and that she peers, seeing silver leaves on silver trees
Through stained glass windows brightly gleam, copper nails in
ancient beams
And by a statue of Sir Thomas Mann, moonlight shines on an old
beer can
From shadowy trees, sparrows peep, deep in silver feathered sleep
Nocturnal cat, she wanders by with silver claw and silver eye
Is this The Palace? Not at all.
It's the garden by St George's Hall…

Seven Ages

Peter Cookson

"All the world's a stage
And all the men and women merely players."

What on earth does the bard mean? Surely not that we are all just acting out, playing the part, the various stages of our lives. Rather it must mean that to the outside observer the phases of our lives are living tableau paraded before our critical eyes.

It is not a kind poem; the poet looks on life with a critical eye, singling out the least likeable features of each age, though not without humour, from puking infant to slippered pantaloons.

No hint of the joys and pleasures of life. Perhaps Shakespeare was depressive or even bipolar!

Annette Butler

The Seven Ages of Man (and Woman)

The familiar poem by William Shakespeare describes in just 28 lines what it is like to go through life. It beautifully and memorably describes life's passage through seven stages.

A modern interpretation, using the idea of a theatre stage where people enter and reappear could also be described as *A Dance to the Music of Time* (a title used by the painter Poussin and by the novelist Anthony Powell). Dancing implies a lightness, enjoyment but it frequently also enjoys concentration, sometimes getting steps right (our actions), but also getting them wrong without meaning to.

So the first stage in life is Birth and the later final stage is Death. "Life is what you make of it" is a truism, and this can be largely true. The infant has to grow up and be well nourished, emotionally and intellectually as well as physically. The second

56

stage or age is School where the child may go eagerly to school, not necessarily reluctantly. Nowadays also likely onwards to college/university. Infinitely more so than in Shakespeare's time is the possibility of stimulating play while learning. We have kindergartens and nursery schools – Shakespeare's lower middle class home had a nurse. The third age is the young adult experiencing unsettling teenage years and then first love. This is an emotionally difficult time. Today we also have the world wide web opening up enormous possibilities of contact via social media such as Facebook and sophisticated phones. Part of this is incessant messaging, not always of a healthy nature and hugely overused; images are all – from photographs often not sufficiently monitored by parents. Friendship now goes well beyond actual friends as in school or college to so-called cyberspace "friends" (very dubious). Fourth stage – not soldiering but working, experiencing life in a deeper way, parenting for many persons with all the learning and passing on of advice that this entails. Shakespeare's Justice could be likened to our mature selves who, hopefully, have acquired some wisdom through our parents and older mentors such as teachers, possibly grandparents. Altogether calmer? The Sixth stage is the ageing process involving some physical deterioration and, if we are really unlucky, the beginnings of mental illness; although modern drugs can help. Our bodies alter. A significant birthday – such as 60 – is a wake up call. We are not keen on seeing ourselves in the mirror. The final seventh stage or age is crunch time even for the physically and mentally fittest of persons. We are living longer, with more leisure opportunities than ever, in theory. But this is almost always going to be easier for the comfortably off than the poorer Pensioner who may well live in a physically deprived area. Those who can have regular holidays see distant grandchildren and children. There are many opportunities for life-long learning. It is a neurologically proved fact that using your brain from learning a new language in mature years to doing crosswords, even walking very regularly help in bodily failing. We keep our teeth (sometimes dentures), use spectacles, survive or best of all Live until Death.

Thelma Thomas

The Seven Ages of Man (Many Parts)

Born no memory – little girl of five, starting school.
Teenage girl – a bit rebellious and thinks she knows it all.
Young woman – out to work, dating, having fun,
up for anything that's going on.

Married woman – went cycling and there he was,
the man I had my eye on. The many laughs
so we made it a thing to last.

Mother – after a while a baby born
then on it went (another four).
Grandmother – what a joy, a little girl.

To be called a Nan was very strange
but I loved it, then it felt like heaven.
(As we ended up with another seven).

Great Grandmother – another baby on the way
so what can I really say,
told I had to have another name as it couldn't be Nan
so after thought and family discussion
I have the label Nana, to my little girl Roxanne.

Angela Bebb

The Seven Ages of Man

Upon reflecting on the words the line that stands out, for me, is "And one man in his time plays many parts." I realize we all play parts, have roles, may have costumes. I decided to look at some of the roles I have participated in.

Skip over childhood, not too happy a time. When I was 18 years old in 1958 I began training as a State Registered Nurse. I donned the uniform and played my part, sometimes not too well. I was also petrified I was going to accidentally kill someone. On my first ward after preliminary training in the classroom a patient (an old lady) called me to her bed and asked why I looked so frightened. I told her my fears and she reassured me by recounting her own experiences in World War 1 when she was a nurse in a casualty clearing station in Passchendaele. It sounded extremely frightening and I cheered up and really enjoyed the rest of my training.

On competition I decided to take up training as a midwife in Edinburgh. I was completely unprepared for the unpleasant attitudes I encountered. On the second day I was there we went to the Ante-natal ward to feel the mother's stomachs to ascertain the lie of the baby. The first lady I attended asked me what the A M stood for on my name badge. I told her Angela Maria. She gave a loud scream and said "you're a papist!" I answered, yes. She shouted to the other ladies: "Don't let this one put her hands on your baby. She's a Papist." I found this very distressing and it happened a number of times. Even on the spell in the district when there were no other midwives to cover. This occurred in the most affluent areas with so-called educated people saying they did not want their babies delivered by an English Catholic.

We had dances once a month in the Nurses Home and I suffered the indignity of partners abandoning me in the middle of the dance floor when they heard my English accent.

59

The training was good but sometimes very sad if a baby was still born or didn't survive very long. I cried at every birth when the baby announced its arrival with its first cry – *I'm here and you'd better take care of me.*

I was glad to leave Edinburgh and off I went to Oxford to train as a Psychiatric nurse. A real culture shock – no uniforms, no badges. It was a Therapeutic Community much ahead of its time. I nearly missed being accepted as we had to spend a couple of days there. I was put in charge of a patient. It was some hours before I realized he was a patient. On the second day at the community meeting my two friends and I were discussed by the group. My friends were accepted immediately but I was rejected as being too haughty and proud. The patient, in whose care I had been, stood up and said *No, she is very shy but very friendly and listens carefully in the small group.* The debate continued and I was eventually accepted thanks to Jason. During my time there my friend and I were persuaded to join the Territorial Army so another uniform and another role. Very exciting and different from making field hospitals in Cornwall to working as a midwife in Germany, to abseiling down cliffs in Anglesey. Eventually I came to Liverpool – another role and back in uniform.

I married and had 5 children. My husband died when my children were aged 9 years to 16 years. I took some time off work, by then I was a CPN. When I returned to work I had my hair done and bought new clothes and was determined to show my colleagues I was OK. I remarried some years later and Andrew and I will celebrate 25 years together this year. A new role again as he has 4 children so became a step-mother. I am now a Grandmother and I have 10 grandchildren and Andrew has 7, so we have seventeen between us.

A couple of years ago I changed roles again when I became an in-patient here at Mossley Hill hospital. Very different on the other side.

And now I'm learning to write with the Mossley Hill writing group.

Ralph Killey

The Seven Stages of Stan

Stan's first stage was bottles and wetting the bed
Then various schools, cramming facts in his head
A job, with some cash, then his urges start buzzin'
That mate, with the legs, went to school with his cousin

Soon there's a wedding, two kids and all that
A mortgage, a cash card a car and a cat
Stan's wife loves the nice things
Her folks were 'well off'

While Stan gets his clothes from The Charity Shop
Sixty looms nigh, his face shows the strain
He sold his gold watch
Sending his kids to Spain

Seventy looms, his vitality's fled!
Then it's back to the bottles and
Wetting the Bed

Margaret Kempson

The Seven Ages of Woman (in the modern idiom)

1
A baby girl, how very nice
she is made of sugar and spice,
ten little fingers and ten little toes,
all complete with a little snub nose.

61

2

Soon Nursery school looms, all too soon,
with climbing frames, slides and see-saws – what a boon.
She takes it all in her stride and makes her mother wait outside.

3

Proper school is next, with a uniform to buy,
in she goes but has a little cry.
She learns to read and write and do her sums
But it is not too long before the next stage comes.

4

Secondary school, lasting a full seven years
lots of exams and plenty of tears.
The teenage spots appear, the crazy fashions bought,
One often wonders though, whether that skirt is too short?

5

Next, off to University, a three year stint.
What to do when she leaves?
Doesn't give the slightest hint.
The degree obtained, a job is found,
at last it seems she is on safe ground.

6

An admiring male catches her eye,
they will soon start courting and could wed by and by.
Marriage may follow and children we hope,
But not too many as it is difficult to cope.

7

Old age beckons and can be a bore,
but it has its compensations and lots more,
free bus travel, free TV licence and help towards fuel bills,
these come in handy if you don't have many ills.
No more work, lots of leisure,
life at this time can be quite a pleasure.

The Time of Our Lives

Peter Cookson

The Eternal City

It is Autumn 1960 and I am 21 on an adventure taking the long tedious train journey to the Eternal City which is just recovering from the Olympics. I am bound for the Venerable English College to begin my study of theology. The College is old – founded in 1262 as a hospice for English pilgrims. It has stood on the same site for eight centuries in the heart of Renaissance Rome. Michelangelo's great Farnese palace is just round the corner; St Peter's is a fifteen minute walk away; nothing later than the sixteenth century. And everywhere relics of ancient Rome poke through the surface. Though it was once the greatest city in the world, all its wonders are within walking distance. The catacombs, the witnesses of early Christian Rome, and small half hidden churches with gorgeous golden mosaics from the third and fourth centuries. Rome is a living and breathing lexicon of world history.

Thelma Thomas

My Best Time

The wedding was stressful, very small. Rod and I did it ourselves. No cake, no drink, we were married at 12 noon on 20th July 1957. We lived in a bedsit off Parkfield Road. It had gaslight. We both worked full time all week and every weekend we cycled and stayed in Youth Hostels overnight. We went mainly into Wales at the week-end but Summer holidays, Easter, Whit and Christmas we went further away – the Isle of Man, Cornwall, Scotland, Derbyshire, Peak District and Yorkshire. Then we bought a second hand mini-bus and we would sleep overnight, roughing it, never on sites – going to Southern Ireland, Isle of Arran, Skye, another time around the coast of Britain, right down to Land's End calling into different places each day. We did hill walking swimming in the sea and lakes. We even tried belly boarding which was a great laugh.

We often brought fish from the fishermen, mackerel or whiting, which we cooked on our Primus stove. Then home to our little flat. We then bought a better van, still old but moving to the terrace house I still live in now. The children now being five in number used to all pile in for our Summer camping in Anglesey for two weeks.

In Winter all off again for days out on a Saturday and Sunday, hope it's snowed. Sledges in trays and a bit of old lino to the slopes of Moel Famau or the Horseshoe Pass. Lots of butties and homemade cake. Then things moved on.

Rod and I started again with all the grandchildren. Days out in the Summer holidays. Picking strawberries and raspberries at PYO farms. The kids all liked going to Beeston Market where they sold pigs and sheep and we all sat in the big barn for the auction of the horses, donkeys and cows. Before the sale started we could go around the pens to see the animals for a pat and a bit of hay. They liked the pigs and piglets the best. The children always laughed when the piglets ran round and nobody could catch them.

All this was my best time with Rod and the children. Lots of adventures. Never a dull moment. It still goes on just as much, but in a different way, now that they have all grown up, some moved out of Liverpool and Rod has gone. I still look for adventures, as my child within often appears.

I feel I was born at the wrong time into the wrong birth family.

Annette Butler

Becoming a Parent

Some people think that the best time of your life is represented by school days. But this is not always the case. For many, the time when they become a parent offers a prospect of a happy and exciting new venture: things can never be the same. As a friend, having her first child aged only 19 said – 'That's when I really grew up." In my case I had my first child in my late 20s when the Midwifery staff had me down on their records as an "elderly primagravature". Really! The second child – the surprise – was born nearly 9 years on when I was 37.

When my daughter, Christina, was born it was the culmination of a certain amount of anxiety and anticipation. The wretched business of feeling bloated and embarrassed by such an intimate exposure of my body ended after several hours. On 3rd July 1975. I was utterly exhausted. Chris, my husband, there throughout, managed not to faint and the look on his face when Christina was safely born was terrific. We laughed and cried a little. I was allowed home several days later.

In contrast to the last decade or so there were no mobile phones back in 1975 with which to take photo to instantly send to relatives and friends. Instead, we waited until baby was sleeping better and I felt more like a human being again! Motherhood/Fatherhood is certainly a learning curve. Sometimes we listened to practical advice, sometimes not. In our case Chris and I sadly lost our mothers some years before we met. We would have loved our Mums to know our daughter, hug her, watch her and – later - her brother grow up. But we did have our fathers and an aunt, albeit a long way off. Taking a child around in a pram, push chair or back carrier often got us talking to perfect strangers. The milestones – walking, speech, increasing awareness were all lovely to watch and usually more than made up for temper tantrums. The innocent squeals of delight at simple things such as mobiles and pets – dogs and cats – gave us, family and friends pleasure. We parents

66

had our small corners to fill with our interests, whilst our child's experiences were ever expanding. Next time around, with our son, Alisdair, it was a bit easier. As he grew as a toddler and on he was often mistaken for a girl as, like me and his sister, he had curly blond hair surrounding a small face and a light build. However, as I had not had a brother I was unused to small males. Despite gender-specific awareness, he gravitated towards toy cars etc but there was Lego equally for girls and boys. Despite ups and downs, parenthood is worth it.

As Roald Dahl said, "It's a funny thing about Mothers and Fathers that even when their own child is the most difficult, disgusting little blister you can ever imagine they still think that he or she is wonderful."

Margaret Kempson

One of the most memorable times of my life was 1966 when we bought our first car. It was a second hand Morris 1000 Traveller. We couldn't afford a new one. It was bliss to go shopping and not to have to wait around for public transport any more. Jim, my husband, also used the car to go to work, which was about 12 miles away so it was a godsend for him. We were also free to visit our relatives in Ashton in Makerfield. We could go for picnics and there was enough room in our car to put up a tray table, as a front passenger seat, folded right up against the dashboard. You could reach over the back seat to pick up your picnic food, which was a great advantage if it happened to rain.

We decided to go on a self-catering holiday and booked a cottage in Pistyll near Nefyn on the Lleyn Peninsula which we saw advertised in the Liverpool Echo. It took us a while to find the cottage as it was in a little backwater but we were all delighted with it. The cottage had a lovely garden next to a field in which there were several horses. As soon as they saw us they came bounding over as our daughter Paula, who was then seven, insisted that we bought carrots every time we went out in order to feed them.

Each day we visited a different beach on the Lleyn, all of which were magnificent. The weather was glorious and so hot that we never needed to wear a jacket.

On our way back to the cottage each evening we used to pass another cottage. The owner always seemed to be standing outside. I recognized him as the detective, Maigret. Every time he saw us he waved like mad but we were too shy to stop and speak to him. However, the landlady of our cottage was very friendly with him and told us that one day he was standing at his gate when a gentleman of the road passed by. He immediately recognized him from his battalion during the second world war. He called him back and invited him in for a meal. The man had fallen on hard times. Rupert Davies paid for accommodation for him in the village and got him to do lots of jobs in the cottage and outside. We thought that was a nice gesture.

My husband Jim and daughter Paula and I enjoyed that holiday so much that we went back again for several years and always had glorious weather.

Colette Williams

I Blocked the Toilet at the MGM Grand

Once upon a time, well 22 years ago to be exact, my big sister Margaret and her husband Chuck treated me to a long weekend in Las Vegas. We were accompanied by their 7 year old grand-daughter, Corin. At that time the hotel was reopening after a massive refurbishment. When my sister told me there were 5000 bedrooms, I thought *she's lived in America too long.* Sorry, Margaret, you were right, so there were also 5000 toilets if we include the public ones.

We all shared one big family room. There were two Queen size beds and I shared one with the 7 year old who slept diagonally

68

so in spite of the space I spent the night hanging on to the edge – but nobody really sleeps in Vegas.

We had an amazing time except from the 7 year old sulking as she wasn't allowed in the gambling area.

The weekend went very quickly. Monday morning arrived and we had to vacate the room by 10 am. This meant a very early start and a substantial breakfast washed down with several cups of coffee. All 4 of us came back from breakfast needing the loo or bathroom (if you're a Yank or married to one). They kindly allowed me to go first, a decision we would all live to regret.

The loo wouldn't flush. Numerous attempts resulted in the water rising and overflowing onto the floor by which time my sister was calling: 'Corin needs to go." I was panic stricken. OMG. I came out of the bathroom. Chuck very gallantly came to the rescue by volunteering to clear the blockage. Where are your marigolds when you need them? By this time my sister was getting slightly hysterical.

I spent the rest of the day feeling mortified, unable to make eye contact with my brother-in-law but it was the sulky 7 year old who came to my aid in a quiet moment she came to my aid, whispering innocently: "you just put too much paper down."

I had the time of my life in Las Vegas and always have a private giggle when I think of those 5000 toilets.

Ralph Killey

Frieda

I worked in the creative Department of the Liverpool Echo newspaper with two colleagues, Don and Colin, we were really good friends and work was a joy.

This little foible of which I write happened in the early nineties when the unions enforced a strict female equality policy. As you can imagine the women reveled in this.

The advertising manager was female and what a female. She was Irish, tall, wore charcoal grey suits with massive shoulders, her hair was jet black and shone like a new Ferrari. She ruled with a rod of steel and Her department functioned perfectly. Her name was Frieda O'Byrne.

However, one day, for a private joke amongst ourselves, I wrote this verse:

Frieda O'Byrne, Frieda O'Byrne
If reincarnated I wish to return
As a hot water bottle in blue or in red
Then filled with hot water, you'll take me to bed.

So what did Colin do? He faxed it to her. To my friend, this was funny. The next thing I know she is at the door of our office demanding to know who wrote the limerick.

So, what did Colin do? He pointed to me and said, "He did." (According to Colin this was hilarious).

To my surprise this giant, ruthless Irish woman, Frieda O'Byrne, turned to me and said in a whisper: "It was very nice, though. Thank you very much."

Life can be happy at times, can't it? Well done, Colin.

Kath Harper

I Had the Time of My Life

What a time I had. The memories will stay,
a 6 week stay in Tampa, Florida,
a road trip to Florida Keys with four beloved women,
in-laws or outlaws in my imagination à la Thelma and Louise.

United by love not tied through blood
We drive in our luxurious 7 seater
through Alligator Alley
arriving at my bucket list destination.

With air boats that seem to float
on the waterways,
a vast eco-system of life,
'walking trees' in Native American mythology,
protected mangroves which give necessary aid
to the precious wildlife.

What a rollercoaster of a ride,
cranes hitching a lift, with unnerving stares
some speedy freewheels into clearings,
raccoons reach out
to take food from our hands.

Then the alligators, gliding in the wild,
magnificent, huge, prehistoric creatures
alongside our boat.

A rub-the-eyes experience.
The Everglades.

And then to SoBe
common parlance for South Beach, Miami
home to the beautiful people.
Versace, such brilliance and such tragedy.
White sands, 50s cars, art deco and bourbon.

Yes, the time of my life
Given through kindness and love.

Alive & Kicking

Annette Butler

Alive and Kicking

This is such a positive idea. Something that everyone should adhere to. It could consist of following something that we've pretty well always done – if we are sensible – a healthy diet, moderate exercise (unless we are one of the growing band of half and full marathon runners some of whom best known to themselves continue to regularly or occasionally participate). Some people even take up such extreme physical activities when they are beyond 60 years old. The oldest marathon runner in the UK is a Sikh gentleman of about 85 years old, who only started in quite recent years.

I have never been able to run, but swim quite regularly, although very slowly. It is always a pleasure to see plump older ladies in particular, and some men swimming with confidence and enjoyment; their body fat is a positive asset in keeping warm in the water: literally alive and kicking.

Of course, it's always a positive to explore new activities with new people, and perhaps a friend or relative. Quite a few are organized by volunteers in libraries and in villages (where opportunities are small compared to cities) – in village halls and, where a village hall does not exist, in a room in a pub. Loneliness can be offset by such and/or by quieter suggestions of participation: visiting the even lonelier in their homes, the disabled – giving gifts to shops etc.,

I am also a great advocate of regular cycling, although it's a more scary activity in increased traffic. I cycle whenever possible, whilst also using buses.

Peter Cookson

Alive & Kicking

Well, alive at least. I'm all too well aware that I'm living on borrowed time.

Nine years ago I suddenly found myself diagnosed with two different cancers and the NHS machine kicked in. It was not, for me, a good time but I have no complaints. The treatment was swift and effective – two major operations within a matter of months – and friendly and caring nursing staff. The second operation called for a long recuperation – three years in a nursing home where again I found great kindness. The experience has left me alive, but not doing a lot of kicking – the long-term psychological effect persists when most of the physical symptoms have worn off. But nine years on, here I am still.

Thelma Thomas

"Mate, you better go."

Rod was at his worst, he couldn't talk and stumbled around. What a job to get him off the ground. I hired a wheelchair from the Red Cross and pushed him to the park. It was cold but I wrapped him up just like a child. Then home again to make us hot chocolate, which we loved. An ambulance came to pick us up as we had an appointment at the Heart Failure clinic; we waited for our lift home in a taxi, which they provided instead of an ambulance (as it didn't turn up) so I got him into the black cab with the help of the driver. Home at last at 8pm at night. I felt so much alone and after months I realized it was just him and me. I rang the hospital, tried the doctors, tried Neurosupport, every day on the phone to somebody or other.

They all asked for our phone number, always going to get

74

back to me, but never did. I started not to trust anyone or what was said to me. Christmas and New Year came and went. All the children and grand-children came around. It was now 2005, Rod's last Christmas. In the following April he closed his eyes as though asleep. He never opened them again. I called the family who took turns to come and go as they all had small children. One of my daughters who is a nurse was on the phone when a doctor came with a piece of paper saying that if I just signed it he would have Rod taken away to hospital – telling me I couldn't cope. Things were said that made me want to attack this doctor but my son took him into the hall and just said to him: "mate, you'd better go."

The Palliative Care team came in, very kind and caring. I felt they really put themselves in my shoes. They had a bed brought in. They washed him and even combed his hair. He was very peaceful. We sat up with him all night. Then he slipped away the next morning at 7.30 am.

The best thing was I kept him at home with all his family around him. He was never left on his own. I hope my own death will be as good as his – but I always feel it won't be.

Thelma Thomas

Kath Harper

60 Years Young

Age is not a number
It's all in the mindset you see
just live for the day
don't wish your life away
so happy and content you will be.

Yes, age is just a number -
Is that a wrinkle or fold I can see?
There are creams and lotions,
serums and potions
so happy and content I will be.

Oh age is just a number
what exactly is that that I see?
The specs are not working,
the reaper is lurking
but restful and peaceful I'll be.

Colette Williams

Hands On

Oh my God, I'm only sixteen,
two weeks since I left school,
my career in nursing has begun
lots of hard work, lots of fun.
The days started early, half past seven,
breakfast served, patients fed,
washes done, beds stripped completely,
fresh sheets put on.

We worked as a team
and young as we were
we started at the bottom,
bums, elbows and heels got extra care
soap and water, methylated spirits
and a little talc to spare
we were so proud,
pressure sores were not allowed.

When the ward work was done
it was off to the sluice.
Bedpans to wash, sterilise and stack,
polished with plate powder
we soon got the knack.

We learned from each other
and study blocks
Lectures from tutors
in white frilly hats
and blue serge frocks.

Something we couldn't learn –
the sixth sense, it developed quietly
would save lives, relieve discomfort
before complaint
nurses who had it –
to the patient, a saint.

Ralph Killey

The Locarno Dance Hall, (Circa 1958)

I can still remember the sting of aftershave
on my adolescent face, and confronting
the big glass doors, with their floral motif,
after the taxi ride to Liverpool's famous *Locarno* dance hall.

The doors were heavy to push,
then the little green ticket, shot up, like a conjuring trick,
from its tiny, chromium trap door
to give you access to wonderland.

The foyer was a symphony in green and white,
groups of lights in clusters of three adorned the walls.
The carpets were lush. You could hear the music of the band,
muted, by the heavy, rich décor
and the green upholstery of the cinema-type seats.

Then came the Coup-de-Theatre.
You pushed open the doors, and there was the Dance Hall.
It was magic itself.
Full of people, of varying ages, all dancing,
to the music and really, really happy.

The band looked like a brand new bathroom,
all white and gleaming.

The drummer sat in a big oyster shell of mother-of-pearl drums.
The brass-section shone like the changing of the guard,
the band leader, with his Shredded Wheat wig,
white Tuxedo and baton,
stood out in front, conducting his maturing musicians.

Everybody danced. There were ponytails,
pink toenails, dyed blond hair everywhere,
prominent checks, Provident Cheques,
New Look skirts, sweaty shirts,
Toni Perms, Easy Terms,
sweets-off-the-ration, cymbals crashin',
no more devastation.
Peace had hit the nation

The band played *Such Sweet Thunder*,
discreet suspenders came asunder,
stocking tops were everywhere,
the girls just laughed
they didn't care.

The shutters had been lifted from our eyes again
And we could all go back to living lives again.

At that moment in a flash of light,
This verse arrived in black and white

A peaceful Europe, Lord we pray
And may it always be that way.

Kath Harper

Alive & Kicking

What a story a face can tell,
the wisdom, the laughter, the love.
A story of life, etched with each line,
each line a chapter or verse,
the shout – we're alive and kicking.

We are alive and kicking,
we're unique and we're tough and we're proud.
We've weathered the storms,
continued on our way.
Sometimes screaming and kicking.

We are alive and kicking,
We're useful and we're kind and we're true.
We've come through some trials,
DVD and T-shirt hooray!
Always alive and kicking.

We are alive and kicking
we're wiser and we're older and we're fun.
We're alive to tell the tale.
Live to fight another day.
Still alive and kicking.

ACKNOWLEDGEMENTS

This is to acknowledge the support of all the members of the Mossley Hill Writing Group, past and present, including Ged Daley our staff support member from Mersey Care NHS Trust during the time the work for this book was developed.

We also want to express our thanks to the Trustees of North End Writers, and staff from Mersey Care who have funded and supported our work especially Carol Bernard, Karen Lawrenson, Margaret Brown, Andrew Garritty and Marion Daniels.

Thanks to Thelma Thomas for the cover art-work.